Calvin and the Reformed Church

Calvin and the Reformed Church

A. M. Fairbairn

WIPF & STOCK · Eugene, Oregon

Wipf and Stock Publishers
199 W 8th Ave, Suite 3
Eugene, OR 97401

Calvin and the Reformed Church
By Fairbairn, A. M.
ISBN 13: 978-1-5326-1608-2
Publication date 2/1/2017
Previously published by Cambridge University Press, 1934

CALVIN AND THE REFORMED CHURCH.

THE Reformation emerges as an inevitable result from the interaction and opposition of many and complex forces. The spirit of the time, even when intending to be its enemy, proved its friend. The Renaissance, which had raised the ancient classical world from its grave, was not in itself opposed to the Catholic Church; but in the reason it educated and the historical temper it formed, in the literature it recovered and the languages it loved, in the imagination it cultivated and the new sense of the beautiful it created, there were forces of subtle hostility to the system which had been built upon the ruins of classical antiquity. Erasmus used his wit to mock the vulgar scholasticism of Luther. But Erasmus more than any man made Protestantism necessary and the Papacy impossible, especially to the grave and reverent peoples of the North. The navigators, who by finding new continents enlarged our notions both of the earth and man, seemed but to add fresh provinces to Rome; but, by moving the centre of social and intellectual gravity from the shores of the Mediterranean to those of the Atlantic, they inflicted on her a fatal wound. Moreover, by the easy acquisition of the wealth which lower races had accumulated, there was begotten in the Latin peoples so fierce and intolerant an avarice that their highest ambitions appeared ignoble, in contrast with the magnanimity and the enterprise of the Teutonic nations that became Protestant.

And just as the history of man's past lengthened and the earth around him broadened and with it his horizon, so the nature beneath him and the heavens above began by telling him their secrets to throw over him their spell. With the new knowledge of nature came new hopes which looked more to the energies that were creating the future than to the authorities that had fashioned the past. Faith in man as man, and not simply as King or noble, as Pope or priest, was reborn; and he appeared as the maker of history and the doer of the deeds that distinguish time. The most famous of the humanists were either themselves poor or sons of poor men, though they might affect, especially in Italy, the Courts of Kings and the palaces of the great, who had patronage as well as power in their hands. The most eminent of the explorers was a Genoese sailor; the best known conqueror was an officer's bastard; the author of the new astronomy was a clerk who never became a priest; the foremost scholar of the day was a child born out of wedlock; the most acute political thinker was a plain Florentine citizen; and the most potent English statesman was the son of a rustic tradesman. And this strenuous individualism found its counterpart in religion; the rights of man in religion were declared; the individual asserted his competence to know and to obey the truth by which he was to be judged.

But the Reformation, at least in its earlier phase, bore also upon its face the image of the man whose genius gave it actual being. Luther had become a Reformer rather by necessity of nature than by choice of will. His peasant descent may have given him a conservative obstinacy which was concentrated and intensified by his narrow scholastic education. No man ever clung with more tender intensity to the customs and beliefs that could be saved from the wreckage of the past. But he did his work as a Reformer the more thoroughly because he did it from nature rather than from choice. It is doubtful if in the whole of history any man ever showed more of the insight that changes audacity into courage. By the publication of his Theses he proclaimed a doctrine of grace that broke up the system which Europe had for centuries believed and obeyed. By burning the papal Bull he defied an authority which no person or people had been able to resist and yet live. By his address to the nobles of the German nation he appealed from ecclesiastical passion and prejudice to secular honour and honesty. By his appearance and conduct at the Diet of Worms he showed that he could act as he had spoken. By his translation of the Bible he spread before the eyes of every religious man the law by which he was bound. And by his marriage he declared the sanctity of the home and the ties which attached man to woman.

But, though Luther was by nature strong and heroic, he was yet so intellectually timid that he could not bear suspense of judgment, even where such suspense was an obvious duty. And so the system he created was, alike in what it sacrificed and what it spared, a splendid example of dialectical adaptation to personal experience. He was indeed so typical a German that his Church suited the German people; but for the same reason it could not live outside Teutonic institutions and the Teutonic mind. He had no constitutional tendency to scepticism, for his convictions did not so much follow or obey as underlie and guide the processes of his logic. Hence he was a man equally powerful in promoting and in resisting change; he stood up against forces that would have overwhelmed a weaker or a smaller man; but as a conservative by nature he professed beliefs that a man of a more consistent intellect would have dismissed, and cherished customs which a more radical reformer would have surrendered. And he was not conscious of any incompatibility among the things he retained or of any coherence between what he gave up and what he spared. Thus he opposed to the authority of the Pope the authority of Holy Scripture; but the Apostle who seemed to ignore or deny his most fundamental belief he was ready to denounce as if he were the Pope. He appealed to the German people to uphold against Rome a Gospel which declared all men to be equal before God; but, when the peasants drew from his first principle an inference which justified their revolt, he sided with the Princes. From his doctrine of Justification by Faith he argued against the papal chair and its claims; but his theory of the Eucharistic Sacrament was more full of mysteries that tax the reason than any of the articles which he regarded as specifically Popish. He held freedom to be the right of every Christian man, and confessed himself bound to accept every consequence which came by legitimate reasoning from the truth he acknowledged; but he refused the right hand of brotherhood to Reformers whose love of freedom, integrity of character, purity of motive, and zeal in the faith were equal to his own.

The longer the Protestant Church lived, the more the Reformer's inconsistencies and the inadequacy of his Reformation became evident; and so a double result followed. On the one side the ancient Church pressed with growing severity upon the revolt and its leaders; and, on the other side, the more eager of the rebellious spirits went forward in search of simpler yet more secure positions. Rome did not indeed understand at once what had happened; but she understood enough to see how Luther and the communities he had founded could best be dealt with. An ancient Church which has governed man for centuries, instructed him, organised and administered his worship, consecrated him from his birth and comforted him in his death, has always an enormous reserve of energy. Man is a being with an infinite capacity for reverence; and it is where he most reveres that he is most conservative and least inclined to change. And consequences soon followed from the Reformation which threatened to limit its scope to the purification of Catholicism, to the restoration of its decayed energies, and to furnishing it with the opportunity of vindicating by policy and argument, by speech and action, its name and its claims. Heresies soon arose in the Protestant as they had arisen in the early Church; the collision of the new thought with the old associations provoked discussion; discussion begat differences; differences became acute antitheses which were hardened into permanence by the very means taken to soften or overcome them. Anabaptism supplied Catholicism with fruitful illustrations of the dangers incident to freedom of thought; the Peasants' War was made to point a moral which appealed to the jealousy of nobles and the ambitions of Kings; the rise of sectaries and the multiplication of sects were employed to set off the excellence of a uniform faith and an infallible Church; the abolition of priesthood and hierarchy was used to unchurch the heretic and deny to his societies both divine authority and sacramental grace. Revival and reaction followed so fast on the heels of reform that, had the Lutheran Church stood alone, neither the eloquence of its founder, nor the sagacity and steadfastness of the Saxon Electors, nor the vigour of Landgrave Philip could have saved it.

But Luther did not exhaust the tendencies that worked for Reform. They were impersonated also in Zwingli. As the one was by disposition and discipline a schoolman who loved the Saints and the Sacraments of the Church, the other was a humanist who appreciated the thinkers of antiquity and the reason in whose name they spoke. Luther never escaped from the feelings of the monk and the associations of the cloister; but Zwingli studied his New Testament with a fine sense of the sanity of its thought, the combined purity and practicability of its ideals, and the majesty of its spirit; and his ambition was to realise a religion after its model, free from the traditions and superstitions of men. It was this that made him so tolerant of Luther, and Luther so intolerant of him. The differences of opinion might have been transcended, but the differences of character were insuperable. The two men stood for distinct ideals and different realities; and as they differed so did their peoples. Differences of political order, geographical situation, and climate could not but reappear in character and in belief as well as in the forms under which these were co-ordinated and expressed. Ecclesiastical order will ever reflect the civil polity prevailing in the region where it is evolved. Thus the Roman Church was built upon the ruins of the Roman Empire; the Eastern patriarchates were organised according to the methods and the offices of Byzantine rule; and the ecclesiastical institutions of the sixteenth century were shaped by the political capacities and usages of the peoples among whom and for whom they were created. Thus the Church adapted to a German kingdom was not suited to the temper and ways of an ancient republic; nor was a system fitted to a despotic State congenial to the genius of a free people. Hence there emerged a twofold difference between the Reformations accomplished by Luther and by Zwingli: one personal, which mainly affected the faith or creed of the Church, another social or civil, which mainly affected its polity. Luther, a schoolman while a Reformer, created out of his learning and experience a faith suited to his personal needs; but Zwingli, a Reformer because a humanist, came to religion through the literature which embodied the mind of Christ and the Church of the Apostles. Hence, the Lutheran Reformation is less radical and complete than the Zwinglian, while its faith is more traditional and less historical and rational. But the differences due to the political order and the civil usage were, if not deeper, yet more divisive. Luther effected his change under an empire and within a kingdom by the help of Princes and nobles; but Zwingli effected his under a republic by the aid of citizens with whom he had to argue as with consciously freeborn men. Both might organise their respective Churches by means of the civil power and in dependence on it; but the civil powers were not the same, the reigning forces being in the one case the law and the princely will, and in the other case the reason and the free choice of men trained in self-government by the usages of centuries. The Lutheran Church was thus more monarchical, the Zwinglian more republican in constitution; the one was constructed by Princes, the other organised by the genius and built by the hands of a free people.

The Reformation, then, could not possibly be expressed in a single homogeneous form. Organisation was a necessity, if the liberty achieved by the movement was to be preserved; but it is a much harder thing to establish an order agreeable to liberty than an order suitable to bondage. When a revolution once begins, authorities, personal or political, may retard or deflect it, but they cannot stop or turn it back. And no revolution leaves man exactly where it found him; the wheel may accomplish its full round, but it never returns to the point whence it started. If, then, man could not go back and must preserve what he had gained, he needed a system that would serve his new mind as Catholicism had served his old. Out of Luther's Reformation came the Church which bears his name; out of Zwingli's the Church which is specially termed the Reformed. This Church was born in Switzerland, but named in France; and the name signified that while it was a Church Protestant and Evangelical like the Lutheran, it was yet ancient and continuous like the Roman, able to change its form or accidents without losing its essence. Being Swiss by birth it was republican in polity and democratic in spirit, a Church freely chosen by a free people and capable of living amid free institutions. But France, in adopting and naming it, made it less national and more cosmopolitan, helping it to realise a character at once more comprehensive and aggressive. Now, the causes of this action may be described as at once general and particular, or national and personal. Of the more general, or national, causes three may here be specified.

French Protestantism was more a lay than a clerical revolt; the men who led and who formed it were without the mental habits or the associations of the priest. At first indeed it was termed, just as if it had been imported from Germany,. "the Lutheran heresy"; but the most notable of the early French martyrs, Louis de Berquin, was a pupil of Erasmus rather than of Luther. The men who made the psalms which the French Protestants loved to sing, were not of the priestly order, while their two most illustrious teachers were both jurists and scholars. It was then but characteristic that the Reformed Church of France should more emphasise moral character and temper than custom or formulated beliefs, and that John Calvin, who was its most creative personality, should not think like a schoolman or appeal to the

Imitatio Christi as Luther had appealed to the *Theologia Germanica*. Its genius was to sacrifice everything which Scripture did not directly sanction and justify; while the genius of the Lutheran Church was to spare everything that Scripture did not expressly forbid. And these differences were felt and resented by the Lutherans long before they were perceived or appreciated by the Catholics; for one of the most tragic things of history is the jealousy which made the Lutherans so fear the Reformed Church that they would at one time rather have seen Rome than Geneva victorious.

Again, the Reformed Church in France had to live in the face of a persecution so severe and a legislation so repressive as to be without parallel in the annals of any civilised country. Certainly, in the case of the early Church the martyrdoms were numerically fewer, while its sufferings were less continuous and its period of persecution not so unbroken and protracted. The Roman amphitheatre was, compared with the Place Maubert, a home of mild humanity; the gay and careless intolerance of Francis I had nothing to learn from pagan hate, while the Inquisition was a fiercer and more pitiless foe than heathenism could have bred. The first martyrdoms took place in 1523 at Meaux and at Paris; by 1526 they had become common. An eye-witness tells us that in six months—1534-5—in Paris alone twenty-seven persons were burned to death. And in 1568, as if to show how the thirst for blood had grown, two Huguenot writers assure us that, during the short peace, in three months more than "ten thousand" people were slain, a statement which the testimony of the Venetian ambassador abundantly confirms. In 1581 a book dedicated to Henry III places the number who had fallen within the few preceding years for the "Religion" at two hundred thousand, and it goes on to enumerate the victims provided by the larger Churches.

These figures may be exaggerated; but the exaggerations, which are those of contemporaries, will seem extravagant only to those who have never looked into the records of congregations and classes. In any case the figures witness to the fierceness of the fires that scorched the Reformed Church in France, and explain if they do not justify "its passion of religious hate," while they drew to it the pity and awakened for it the admiration of all its sister and daughter communities. To define policy and shape character in their own and other lands, for their own and later ages, has ever been the prerogative of the persecuted. And this prerogative the Huguenot has exercised as a splendid revenge. He had no opportunity of becoming a loyal citizen; the State would not allow him. L'Hôpital laid down the principle that there could be no civil unity where there was religious dissension; and that the city which allowed its citizens to disagree in their theological beliefs could know no peace. While he urged the sectaries to cultivate charity, and cease to use the "*mots diaboliques*" which they flung at each other, and to employ instead the truest and most characteristic of names—"Christian," yet his thought translated into law rendered, so far as the Huguenot was concerned, duty to the State and duty to conscience incompatible. And the tragic struggle in which the Huguenot was engaged made him a heroic and a potent figure. What the French Revolution did later for the European peoples, the Huguenot did for Protestantism. He made his faith illustrious; his example became infectious, and the Churches of other lands loved to emulate the Reformed Church of France. And this effect was at once intensified and heightened by the expulsive power of the anti-Protestant legislation. It drove men out of France without expelling their love of France; they only loved her the more that she had made them fugitives for conscience' sake. Men like John Calvin and Theodore Beza did not cease to be sons of France though they became citizens of Geneva; and they used their foreign citizenship to serve their mother land more effectually than they could have done in any of her own cities. The Protestants failed in France, yet it is doubtful whether without their failure there the Reformed Church could have prospered. The events that so tended to define its creed and demeanour, helped it to fight its battles the more bravely.

Finally, the Reformed Church as organised by the French mind belongs essentially to the second Protestant generation, and its distinctive note was an enlarged historical knowledge and a clarified historical sense. The feeling for religion was in the second generation not less strong than in the first; but it knew better the problem to be solved and had become more conscious of the many and complex factors required for its solution. The new literature had almost nothing to do with determining the minds and motives of the earlier Reformers; but determined almost exclusively those of the later. With the exception of Melanchthon no Lutheran of the front rank came from the humanists, but all the creative minds of the Reformed Church were children of the Renaissance. The problem as they saw it was historical and literary as well as religious. The Old Testament which Reuchlin had recovered and the New Testament which Erasmus had published and interpreted enabled them to study both the religion which Christ had found and the religion which He had made; the Apostolic writings showed how the men who knew Him or who knew those who knew Him understood and tried to realise His mind. Their own experience had set them face to face with a Church and system which claimed to express the mind of the Apostles and to represent the apostolical society. They were not curious and scientific enquirers who wished to discover how the one had become the other, or how the twin laws of continuity and change had fulfilled themselves in history; they were convinced and sincere religious men, who studied first the Scriptures to find the idea of Christ, and then their own times to see whether it had been and how it could be realised.

There was thus an objectivity in the Reformed ideal which was absent from the Lutheran; a greater thoroughness, a more comprehensive spirit, a more conscious and coherent endeavour to repeat and reflect the Apostolic age. The Reformed Church was not built to meet the exigencies of an expanding personal experience, but articulated throughout according to a consciously conceived idea. It bore indeed even more than the Lutheran the impress of a single mind; but then that mind was as typical of France and the second Protestant generation as Luther was typical of Germany and the first; and it had come by a very different process and way to the convictions which drove it into action. Calvin, like Zwingli, was a humanist before he became a Reformer, and what he was at first he never ceased to be. On the intellectual side, as a scholar and thinker, his affinities were with Erasmus, though on the religious side they were rather with Luther; indeed, Calvin can hardly be better described than by saying that his mind was the mind of Erasmus, though his faith and conscience were those of Luther. He had the clear reason and the open vision of the one, but the religious fire and moral passion of the other. The conscience made the intellect constructive, the intellect made the conscience imperious—at once individual, architectonic, and collective. In Calvin the historical sense of the humanist, and the spiritual passion of the Reformer, are united; he knows the sacred literature which his reason has analysed, while his imagination has seen the Apostolic Church as an ideal which his conscience feels bound to realise. There was rigorous logic in all he did; dialectic governed him, from the humanism which furnished his premises to the religion which built up his conclusions. This is the man whom we must learn to know, if we would understand the Reformed Church, what it did, and what it became in his hands.

The personal cause, then, which most of all contributed to the creation of the Reformed Church, as history knows it, is John Calvin; and him we must here attempt to understand from two points of view: first, that of descent and education; secondly, that of the place and sphere in which he did his work.

Calvin was born on July 10, 1509, at Noyon, near Paris. It was the year when Henry VIII had succeeded to the English throne; when Colet was meditating the formation of a school which was to bear the name of the Apostle whom he loved; when Erasmus, learned and famous, was in Rome, holding high argument with the Cardinal de' Medici; when Luther attained the dignity of *Sententiarius*, and had been called to Wittenberg; and when Melanchthon, though only a boy of thirteen, matriculated at Heidelberg. Calvin's ancestors had been bargemen on the Oise; but his father, Gérard Calvin, had forsaken the ancestral craft, and had sometime before 1481 moved from Pont l'Évêque to Noyon, where he had prospered, and had in due course become *Notaire apostolique, Procureur fiscal du Comté, Scribe en Cour d'Église, Secrétaire de l'Évesché, et Promoteur du Chapitre.* He married Jeanne le Franc, the daughter of a well-to-do and retired innkeeper, described by a Catholic historian as a "most beautiful woman," and by a local tradition as "remarkably devout." Beza says that the family was honourable and of moderate means; and he adds that the father was a man of good understanding and counsel, and therefore much in request among the neighbouring nobility. To this couple were born four sons and two daughters, John being the second son. The father, who intended the boy for the Church, had the successful man's belief in a liberal education, and obtained for him, just as the modern father seeks a scholarship or exhibition, first, the revenues of a chapel in the cathedral, and some years later those of a neighbouring curacy. Among the local gentry was the distinguished family of Montmor. One of them, Charles de Hangest, was from 1501 to 1525 Bishop of Noyon; and his nephew Jean held the same episcopate for the succeeding fifty-two years. This Jean quarrelled lustily with the Chapter, which disliked his manners, his dress, his beard, and possibly also the tolerance of heresy which made him "*suspect dans sa foi et odieux à l'Église et à l'État.*" It is probable that his friendship with this episcopal race helped Gérard to rise, and also hastened his fall. Whatever the cause—whether financial embarrassments, personal attachments, dubious orthodoxy, or all three combined—his later years were more troubled than his earlier; and he died in 1531 under the Ban of the Church. There is no evidence of any latent Protestantism either in him or in his family at this time, though four years later John had become the hope of the stern and unbending Reformers, and within five years the eldest son Charles had died as *une âme damnée*, for he refused on his deathbed to receive the Sacraments of the Church.

Calvin's education began in the bosom of the Montmor family, not indeed as a matter of charity, but, as Beza tells us, at the charges of his father; and though Calvin never forgot that he was "*unus de plebe homuncio*," yet he was always grateful for the early associations which gave to his mind and bearing a characteristic distinction. In 1523 he was sent to Paris, where he entered as a student of Arts the College de la Marche, whence he passed, for his later and more special studies, to the College de Montaigu. The University of Paris was old and famous, but its then state was not equal to its age or its fame. Erasmus describes how the students were mobbed and hunted on the streets, the sort of houses, no better than *lupanaria*, which they frequented or lodged in, the filthy language they heard or used, the still filthier deeds they were expected to do or suffer. Rabelais' Panurge comes to Paris skilled in a host of tongues, but *malfaisant, pipeur, beuveur, bateur de pavéz, ribleur*, averse to no form of mischief or pruriency. James Dryander, brother of Francis, one of Calvin's innumerable correspondents, describes the *præceptorculi* and the *magistelli* of the University as amazing the students by the impudence and ineptitude with which they explained authors whom they did not understand. And how did the boy of fourteen conduct himself in this, to him, strange atmosphere? We need not trust the admiring or depreciative narratives of later men; but we may judge the lad by the friends he made.

Foremost among these stand the four Cops. The father, Guillaume Cop, the King's physician, correspondent of Reuchlin and friend of Erasmus, who praised him as of medicine the *vindex et antistes*, and as *Musarum cultor*, and the sons—Jean, who became a canon of the Church; Nicolas, who in 1530 became a professor of philosophy, and in 1533 delivered as Rector of the University an address which made both him and Calvin famous; and the youngest of the brothers, Michel, who followed Calvin to Geneva and became a Protestant pastor. Beside the Cops there stands another Erasmian, Guillaume Budé, of whom Calvin in his earliest work spoke as "*primum rei literariae decus et columen, cuius beneficio palmam eruditionis hodie sibi vendicat nostra Gallia.*" One of the regents of the College de la Marche was Mathurin Cordier, an enthusiastic teacher who loved learning and learners, and whose keen eye saw the rich promise hidden in his new scholar. The relations of master and pupil were almost ideal. Calvin never ceased to regard Cordier with affection, dedicating to him in profound but reserved gratitude one of his commentaries; Cordier ever respected Calvin, and showed his respect by becoming, like him, a Protestant, and following him to Geneva, where he died, though thirty-two years Calvin's senior, in the same year as his quondam pupil.

And here, perhaps, we may most fitly glance at the commonest of all the charges brought against Calvin. He is said to have been even then austere, severe, harsh, intolerant, inaccessible to the softer emotions, well entitled to bear the name which the playful companions of his youth gave him, "the Accusative." But how stand the facts? There is no scholar of his time more distinguished by his willingness to serve friends or his power to attach and bind them to himself by bands of steel. Of the de Montmors, with whom he was educated, almost all, in spite of high ecclesiastical connexions and hopes, became Protestants, while to his old fellow-pupil, Claude, he dedicated the firstfruits of his literary genius. The Cops and Cordier have already been noticed; and, though Budé did not himself cease to be a Catholic, yet his wife and family all became Protestants, five of them on his death in 1549 seeking refuge in Geneva. Another early teacher whom Calvin deeply revered, expressing his reverence in one of his most characteristic dedications, was the Lutheran Melchior Wolmar, to whom he owed his introduction to the Greek language and literature. But if one would understand the young Calvin, one must study him as revealed in his letters to friends and companions like François Connan, whom he describes as the wisest and most learned of men, whom he trusts above all others, and whose advice he rejoices to follow; or François Daniel, whom Calvin salutes as "*amice incomparabilis,*" or as "*frater et amice integerrime*"; or Nicolas du Chemin, whom he rallies on his literary ambitions, and addresses as "*mea vita charior.*" The man is here revealed as nature made him, and before he had to struggle against grim death for what was dearer to him than life; affectionate and delicate, not in body, but in spirit.

In 1528 Calvin's father, perhaps illuminated by the disputes in his Cathedral Chapter, discovered that the law was a surer road to wealth and honour than the Church, and decided that his son should leave theology for jurisprudence. The son, nothing loth, obeyed, and left Paris for Orleans, possibly, as he descended the steps of the College de Montaigu, brushing shoulders with a Spanish freshman named Ignatius Loyola. In Orleans Calvin studied law under Pierre de l'Estoile, who is described as *jurisconsultorum Gallorum facile princeps*, and as eclipsing in classical knowledge Reuchlin, Aleander, and Erasmus; and Greek under Wolmar, in whose house he met for the first time Theodore Beza, then a boy about ten years of age. After a year in Orleans he went to Bourges, attracted by the fame of the Italian jurist Alciati, whose ungainliness of body and speech and vanity of mind his students loved to satirise and even by occasional rebellion to chasten. In 1531 Gérard Calvin died and his son in 1532 published his first work, a Commentary on Seneca's *De Clementia*. His purpose has been construed by the light of his later career; and some have seen in the book a veiled defence of the Huguenot martyrs, others a cryptic censure of Francis I, and yet others a prophetic dissociation of himself from Stoicism. But there is no mystery in the matter; the work is that of a scholar who has no special interest in either theology or the Bible. This may be statistically illustrated: Calvin cites twenty-two Greek authors and fifty-five Latin, the quotations being most abundant and from many books; but in his whole treatise there are only three Biblical texts expressly cited, and those from the Vulgate. The man is cultivated and learned, writes elegant Latin, is a good judge of Latinity, criticises like any modern the mind and style, the knowledge and philosophy, the manner, the purpose, and the ethical ideas of Seneca; but the passion for religion has not as yet penetrated as it did later into his very bones. Erasmus is in Calvin's eyes the ornament of letters, though his large edition of Seneca is not all it ought to have been; but even Erasmus could not at twenty-three have produced a work so finished in its scholarship, so real in its learning, or so wide in its outlook.

What gives the book significance is the nature that shines through it; the humanist is a man with a passion for conduct, moral, veracious, strenuous, who has loved labour and bestowed it without grudging on the classical writer with whom he has most affinity. Of the twin pillars of Roman philosophy and eloquence Cicero is for him an easy first, but Seneca is a clear second. Calvin is here at once a jurist and a scholar, but amid his grammatical, literary, and historical discussions—every phrase and idea interpreted being illustrated from classical authorities— he speaks his mind with astonishing courage concerning the qualities and faults of kings and judges, States and societies. He bids monarchs remember that their best guardians are not armies or treasuries, but the fidelity of friends and the love of subjects. Arrogance may be natural in a prince, but it does not therefore cease to be an evil. A sovereign may ravage like a wild beast, but his reign will be robbery and oppression, and the robber is ever the enemy of man. Cruelty makes a king execrable; and he will be loved only as he imitates the gentleness of God. And so clemency is true humanity; it is a heroic virtue, hard to practise, yet without it we cannot be men. And he uses it to qualify the Stoic ethics; pity is not to him a disease of the soul, it is a sign and condition of health; no good man is without pity; the Athenians did well when they built an altar to this virtue. Cicero and even Juvenal teach us that it is a vice not to be able to weep. And the doctrine becomes in Calvin's hands social; man pitiful to men will be sensible of their rights and his own duties. Conscience is necessary for us, but his good name is necessary to our neighbour; and we must not so follow our conscience as to injure his good name. We ought so to follow nature that others may see the reason in the nature that we follow. He can be humorous, and laughs at the ridiculous ceremonies which accompanied the apotheosis of Caesar, or at the soothsayers who prophesied without smiling; but he is usually serious and grave, criticising Seneca for speaking of Fortune instead of God, and the Stoics for doctrines which make human nature good, yet isolate the good man from mankind. The ethics of the Stoics he loved, but not their metaphysics; their moral individualism and their forensic morality he admired, but the defects of their social and collective ideals he deplored and condemned. The humanist is alive with moral and political enthusiasm, but the Reformer is not yet born.

The events of the next few months are obscure, but we know enough to see how forces, internal and external, were working towards change. In the second half of 1532 and the earlier half of 1533 Calvin was in Orleans, studying, teaching, practising the law, and acting in the University as Proctor for the Picard nation; then he went to Noyon, and in October he was once more in Paris. The capital was agitated; Francis was absent, and his sister, Margaret of Navarre, held her Court there, favouring the new doctrines, encouraging the preachers, the chief among them being her own almoner, Gérard Roussel. Two letters of Calvin to Francis Daniel belong to this date and place; and in them we find a changed note. One speaks of "the troublous times," and the other narrates two events: first, it describes a play "pungent with gall and vinegar," which the students had performed in the College of Navarre to satirise the Queen; and secondly, the action of certain factious theologians who had prohibited Margaret's *Mirror of a Sinful Soul*. She had complained to the King, and he had intervened. The matter came before the University, and Nicolas Cop, the Rector, had spoken strongly against the arrogant doctors and in defence of the Queen, "mother of all the virtues and of all good learning." Le Clerc, a parish priest, the author of the mischief, defended his performance as a task to which he had been formally appointed, praising the King, the Queen as woman and as author, contrasting her book with "such an obscene production" as *Pantagruel*, and finally saying that the book had been published without the approval of the faculty and was set aside only as "liable to suspicion."

Two or three days later, on November 1, 1533, came the famous rectorial address which Calvin wrote, and Cop revised and delivered; and which shows how far the humanist had travelled since April 4, 1532, the date of the *De Clementia*. He is now alive to the religious question, though he has not carried it to its logical and practical conclusion. Two fresh influences have evidently come into his life, the New Testament of Erasmus and certain sermons by Luther. The exordium of the address reproduces, almost literally, some sentences from Erasmus' *Paraclesis*, including those which unfold his idea of the *philosophia Christiana*; while the body of it repeats Luther's exposition of the Beatitudes and his distinction between Law and Gospel, with the involved doctrines of Grace and Faith. Yet "*Ave gratia plena*" is retained in the exordium; and at the end the peacemakers are praised, who follow the example of Christ and contend not with the sword but with the word of truth.

This address enables us to seize Calvin in the very act and article of change; he has come under a double influence. Erasmus has compelled him to compare the ideal of Christ with the Church of his own day; and Luther has given him a notion of Grace which has convinced his reason and taken possession of his imagination. He has thus ceased to be a humanist and a Papist, but has not yet become a Reformer. And a Reformer was precisely what his conscience, his country, and his reason compelled him to become. Francis was flagrantly immoral, but a fanatic in religion; and mercy was not a virtue congenial to either Church or State. Calvin had seen the Protestants from within; he knew their honesty, their honour, the purity of their motives, and the integrity of their lives; and he judged, as a jurist would, that a man who had all the virtues of citizenship ought not to be oppressed and treated as unfit for civil office or even as a criminal by the State. This is no conjecture, for it is confirmed by the testimony he bears to the influence exercised over him by the martyred Étienne de la Forge. He thus saw that a changed mind meant a changed religion, and a changed religion a change of abode. Cop had to flee from Paris, and so had Calvin.

In the May of 1534 he went to Noyon, laid down his offices, was imprisoned, liberated, and while there he seems to have finally renounced Catholicism. But he feared the forces of disorder which lurked in Protestantism, and which seemed embodied in the Anabaptists. Hence at Orleans he composed a treatise against one of their favourite beliefs, the sleep of the soul between death and judgment. Conscious personal being was in itself too precious, and in the sight of God too sacred, to be allowed to suffer even a temporary lapse. But to serve the cause he loved was impossible with the stake waiting for him, its fires scorching his face, and kindly friends endangered by his presence. And so in the winter of 1534 he retired from France and settled at Basel.

Aeneas Sylvius had once described Basel as a city which venerated images, but cared little for science, and had no wish to know letters; and when he became Pope he founded there a University which effected a more marvellous change than he could have anticipated. Erasmus chose Basel as his residence from 1514 to 1529; and here his New Testament and his editions of the great Latin Fathers were printed by John Froben, who joined to the soul of an artist the enterprise of a merchant. When Froben died Erasmus forsook Basel; but as the end drew near he came back, just as Calvin was finishing his *Institutio*, to die in the city which had been the scene of his most arduous and fruitful labours. And if the zeal for learning at Basel was strong, the zeal for religion was no less. As early as 1517 Capito had refused to celebrate the Mass, and had preached in the spirit of Luther. Here Œcolampadius had learned from humanism a sweet reasonableness that won the respect of Erasmus, yet ideas so radical that they placed him beside Zwingli at Marburg, and made him so preach against the images which the city used to venerate that the rabble hastened to insult and break them. Erasmus, who described the event in more than one letter, marvelled in his satirical way that "not a solitary Saint lifted a blessed finger" to work a protecting or retributory miracle that should stay or avenge the damage. Calvin did not reach the city which Œcolampadius had changed till three years after his death; but the Reformer found it guided by men who were just as congenial: Oswald Myconius, the chief pastor and preacher, who, even amid notable differences, continued ever a personal friend and admirer; Simon Grynaeus, a learned Grecian, with whom he then and later discussed, as he himself tells us, how best to study, to translate, and to interpret the Scriptures; Sebastian Munster, professor of Hebrew, just seeing through the press his *Biblia Hebraica*, praised in public as *Germanorum Esdras et Strabo*, and affectionately known in private as "the Rabbi," a master at whose feet Calvin could sit without shame; Thomas Platter, once a poor and vagrant scholar, then professor of Greek, but now a printer from whose press the *Institutio* was soon to issue, though owing to financial straits not so soon as its anxious author would have liked. Besides the residents, famous visitors came to Basel: from Zurich Henry Bullinger, who was there just at this time, discussing the terms of the First Helvetic Confession, and twenty-one years later reminded Calvin of their meeting; and Conrad Pellican, who saw the dying Erasmus and heard great things of a certain John Calvin, a Frenchman who had dared to write plain and solid truth to the French King.

Now a city where Protestantism reigned, where learning flourished, and where men so unlike as Erasmus and Farel—the fervid preacher of Reform—could do their work unhindered, was certain to make a deep impression on a fugitive harassed and expatriated on account of religion; and the impression it made can be read in the *Christianae Religionis Institutio*, and especially in the prefatory Letter to Francis I. The *Institutio* is Calvin's positive interpretation of the Christian religion; the Letter is learned, eloquent, elegant, dignified, the address of a subject to his sovereign, yet of a subject who knows that his place in the State is as legal, though not as authoritative, as the sovereign's. It throbs with a noble indignation against injustice, and with a noble enthusiasm for freedom and truth. It is one of the great epistles of the world, a splendid apology for the oppressed and arraignment of the oppressors. It does not implore toleration as a concession, but claims freedom as a right. Its author is a young man of but twenty-six, yet he speaks with the gravity of age. He tells the King that his first duty is to be just; that to punish unheard is but to inflict violence and perpetrate fraud. Those for whom he speaks are, though simple and godly men, yet charged with crimes that, were they true, ought to condemn them to a thousand fires and gibbets. These charges the King is bound to investigate, for he is a minister of God, and if he fails to serve the God whose minister he is then he is a robber and no King. The lowliness of the men has as its counterpart the majesty of their beliefs, for the sake of which " *alii nostrum vinculis constringuntur, alii virgis caeduntur, alii in ludibrium circumducuntur, alii proscribuntur, alii saevissime torquentur, alii fuga elabuntur, omnes rerum angustia premimur, diris exsecrationibus devovemur, maledictis laceramur, indignissimis modis tractamur.*" Then he asks, " Who are our accusers?" and he turns on the priests like a new Erasmus, who does not, like the old, delight in satire for its own sake or in a literature which scourges men by holding up the mirror to vice; but who feels the sublimity of virtue so deeply that witticisms at the expense of vice are abhorrent to him. He takes up the charges in detail: it is said that the doctrine is new, doubtful, and uncertain, unconfirmed by miracles, opposed to the Fathers and ancient custom, schismatical and productive of schism, and that its fruits are sects, seditions, licence. On no point is he so emphatic as the repudiation of the personal charges: the people he pleads for have never raised their voice in faction or sought to subvert law and order; they fear God sincerely and worship Him in truth, praying even in exile for the royal person and House.

The book which this address to the King introduces is a sketch or programme of reform in religion. The first edition of the *Institutio* is distinguished from all later editions by the emphasis it lays, not on dogma, but on morals, on worship, and on polity. Calvin conceives the Gospel as a new law which ought to be embodied in a new life, individual and social. What came later to be known as Calvinism may be stated in an occasional sentence or implied in a paragraph, but it is not the substance or determinative idea of the book. The problem discussed has been set by the studies and the experience of the author; he has read the New Testament as a humanist learned in the law, and he has been startled by the contrast between its ideal and the reality which confronts him. And he proceeds in a thoroughly juridical fashion, just as Tertullian before him, and as Grotius and Selden after him. Without a document he can decide nothing; he needs a written law or actual custom; and his book falls into divisions which these suggest. Hence his first chapter is concerned with duty or conduct as prescribed by the Ten Commandments; his second with faith as contained in the Apostolic symbol; his third with prayer as fixed by the words of Christ; his fourth with the Sacrament as given in the Scriptures; his fifth with the false sacraments as defined by tradition and enforced by Catholic custom; and his sixth with Christian liberty or the relation of the ecclesiastical and civil authorities. But though the book is, as compared with what it became later, limited in scope and contents—the last edition which left the author's hand in 1559 had grown from a work in six chapters to one in four books and eighty chapters—yet its constructive power, its critical force, its large outlook impress the student. We have here none of Luther's scholasticism, or of Melanchthon's deft manipulation of incompatible elements; but we have the first thoughts on religion of a mind trained by ancient literature to the criticism of life.

In the second edition published in 1539 his old admirations reassert themselves. Plato is there described as of all philosophers "*religiosissimus et maxime sobrius*"; and Aristotle, Themistius, Cicero, Seneca, and other classical writers are quoted in a way that finds a parallel in no theological book of the period. But in this first edition he is too much in earnest, and writes too directly, to adorn his pages with classical references; though in his style, in his argument, in his deduction of all things from God, and in his correlation of our knowledge of God and of man, in his emphasis on morals, in his sense for conduct and love of freedom, the classical spirit is living and active. Thus, in his ideas of Christian liberty we can trace the student of Seneca, as in his appreciation of law and order we see the Roman jurist. He dislikes equally tyranny and licence. Liberty is said to consist in three things: freedom from the law as a means of acceptance with God, the spontaneous obedience of the justified to the Divine will, and freedom either to observe or neglect those external things which are in themselves indifferent. He specially insists on this last; since without it there will be no end to superstition and the conscience will enter a long and inextricable labyrinth whence escape will be difficult. The Church is the elect people of God, and must, if it is to do its work in the world, obey Him. But it can obey only as it has control over its own destinies and authority over its own members. It will not err in matters of opinion if it is guided by the Holy Spirit and judges according to the Scriptures. Magistrates are ordained of God, and ought to be obeyed, even though wicked; but here a most significant exception is introduced. God is King of Kings; when He opens His mouth, He alone is to be heard; it were worse than foolish to seek to please men by offending Him. We are subject to our rulers, but only in Him; if they command what He has forbidden, we must fear God and disobey the King.

The *Institutio* bears the date "*Mense Martio; Anno* 1536"; but Calvin, without waiting till his book was on the market, made a hurried journey to Ferrara, whose Duchess, Renée, a daughter of Louis XII, stood in active sympathy with the Reformers. The reasons for this brief visit are very obscure; but it may have been undertaken in the hope of mitigating by the help of Renée the severity of the persecutions in France. On his return Calvin ventured, tradition says, to Noyon, probably for the sake of family affairs; but he certainly reached Paris; and, while in the second half of July making his way into Germany, he arrived at Geneva. An old friend, possibly Louis du Tillet, discovered him, and told Farel; and Farel, in sore straits for a helper, besought him, and indeed in the name of the Almighty commanded him, to stay. Calvin was reluctant, for he was reserved and shy, and conceived his vocation to be the scholar's rather than the preacher's; but the entreaties of Farel, half tearful, half minatory, prevailed. And thus Calvin's connexion with Geneva began.

With the ancient and medieval history of Geneva we have here no concern; it will be enough if we briefly indicate those peculiarities of its constitution which gave Calvin his opportunity, and so much of its history as will explain the condition in which he found it.

Ethnographically Geneva was connected with both the Teutonic and the Latin races; by language it was French, by religious interests and associations Italian, by political instincts and affinities Swiss, by commercial and industrial genius German. In the thirteenth century its civil superior had been a Count of Burgundy; in the fifteenth century and early sixteenth he had been long superseded by the Dukes of Savoy. And the supersession was inevitable, for Geneva occupied a corner of the Savoyard country; and, as an old chronicler has it, the bells of the city were heard by more Savoyards than citizens. Its constitution, at once hierarchical, feudal, and democratic, so balanced parties, whose interests were seldom compatible, as to put a premium on agitation and intrigue. These parties were the Bishop, the Vicedom, or civil overlord, and the citizens.

The Bishop was the sovereign of the city, elected originally by the clergy and laity jointly, later by the Cathedral Chapter, though customs significant of the older time continued to be observed. Thus the mere vote of the Chapter did not constitute the Bishop lord of the State; the election had further to be endorsed by the citizens, who accompanied the Bishop in solemn procession to the Cathedral, where before the altar and in the presence of clergy and people he swore on the open Missal that he would preserve their laws, their liberties, and their privileges. As sovereign he issued the coinage, imposed the customs, was general of the forces, and supreme judge in both civil and ecclesiastical causes. In criminal cases he exercised the prerogative of mercy, and endorsed or remitted penalties. The Cathedral Chapter formed his Council and represented him in his absence. It constituted a permanent aristocracy, and sat as a sort of spiritual peerage in the city Council. Certain castles and demesnes were assigned to the Bishop, in order that he might be as sovereign in appearance and in dignity as he was in law and in fact.

The Vicedom was captain of the Church, commissioned to repress violence in the city and to defend it from external attacks, to act in the less important civil and criminal cases, and to carry out the penalties which the law pronounced. He was not reckoned a citizen, and stood sponsor for all the foreigners who enjoyed the hospitality of Geneva. While in theory the Bishop's vassal, yet, as a matter of fact and for reasons which neither he nor the city was allowed to forget, the office had become hereditary in the House of Savoy; but as the Duke could not himself reside, his duties were discharged by two lieutenants, whose functions were carefully defined and delimited. In a word, the civil over-lord was the minister of his ecclesiastical superior; but the superior tended to become the puppet of the minister.

Apart from both stood the citizens in an order of their own. The general Council of the city, composed of the whole of the citizens, *i.e.* all the heads of families, met at the summons of the great bell twice each year to transact business affecting the community as such, to elect the four Syndics and the Treasurer, to conclude alliances, to proclaim laws, to fix the prices of wine and of grain. The Syndics represented the municipal independence as against the sovereignty of the Bishop and the power of the Vicedom. To them the greater criminal jurisdiction was entrusted, and they were responsible for good order within the city from sunset to sunrise. They were assisted by the Smaller Council, composed of twenty qualified citizens; and if any event too responsible for it to handle occurred, the Council of Sixty could be called, which was composed of the representatives of the several districts and the most experienced and respectable citizens. Later, and just before the

Reformation, the Council of Two Hundred was established in order that Geneva might be assimilated to the Swiss Cantons whose help it invoked.

A State so constituted and governed could hardly escape from the consciousness that it was a Church, or feel otherwise than as if the ecclesiastic at its head made its acts and legislation ecclesiastical. The spiritual offices were made secular without the secular offices becoming spiritual; in other words, the clergy were assimilated to the laity, while the laity did not correspond to the clerical ideal. The priests dressed and armed like the people, played and fought with them, behaved more like examples of worldliness than teachers of the Gospel; in a word, sinned and lived like citizens of Geneva. The decay of clerical morals was not peculiar to Geneva, though it must be noted as a main factor of the situation there. Kampschulte, here a reluctant witness, declares that the Bishop had become a humiliation to the Church and a degradation to the clergy; and he cites the case of the old priest who, when ordered to put away his mistress, replied that he was quite ready to obey, provided all his brethren were treated with the same severity. But the constitution acted on the collective even more subtly than on the personal consciousness. The Council legislated, disciplined, and excommunicated as if the State were a Church, or, what may be the same thing, as if there were no Church in the State. The extent to which a man could sin and yet remain a citizen was a matter of statutory regulation: no citizen was allowed to keep more than one mistress, and every convicted adulterer was banished. The prostitutes had a quarter where they dwelt, special clothing which they wore, and a "queen" who was responsible for the good order of her community. The clergy were a kind of moral police, responsible for the citizens and to the city; and so their deterioration meant a moral decline.

But a more obvious and, so far as our immediate point is concerned, a more serious consequence was this: every ecclesiastical question tended to become civil, and every civil question to become ecclesiastical. A constitution has a way of working in a fashion either better or worse than, considered *à priori*, would have seemed possible; and this because the people are ever a greater factor of harmony or disorder than the laws they live under. Hence, so long as Geneva was inspired by one spirit, the anomalies of the constitution did not breed discontent; but, when new energies and new ambitions awoke, these anomalies became fruitful of disaster to the State. So long as the Bishop and the people had common aims and interests, loyalty to both was easy; but, the moment the interests of the Bishop looked in an opposite direction from those of the people, the situation became difficult. For loyalty to the Bishop as head of the State meant loyalty to the Church of which he was head; but loyalty to the people as the chief constituent of the State became disloyalty to the Bishop as head both of Church and city. How this situation arose in Geneva, what it signified and whither it tended, subsequent events will show.

The determining factors of the situation were thus two, the Bishop and the Duke. The Bishop stood for an ideal which he was not always either able or willing to realise; the Duke, who was his vice-lord, stood for an interest whose strength grew with its years, and created the energy needed for its own realisation. The function of a Bishop's Vicar did not satisfy the House of Savoy; it wanted to be master in its own right, and sit in Geneva facing the ultramontane kingdoms, as it sat in Turin and faced the cismontane principalities and cities. And so began the game of intrigue in which the House has always been a skilled performer; and the Bishop was played off against the people, and the people against the Bishop. But it is harder to capture a whole city than a single person; it is easier to annex an exalted office than to control a whole population, a multitude of impulsive souls, singly accessible to incalculable yet imperious ideas. So the House concentrated itself on the Bishop; intrigued with the Chapter which elected; intrigued with Rome which approved; prevailed with both, and got its creatures appointed, men who would do its will and forget their office and its duties. A chronicler says that "Duke and Bishop, like Herod and Pilate, stood united against the city." The Bishop he means is the Bastard of Savoy, appointed 1513, a man of notoriously immoral conduct, and in everything the unscrupulous instrument of the ducal policy. He lived ignobly, but served his House as best he could; and in a moment of remorse, on his death-bed in 1522, he admonished his successor, Pierre de la Baume, thus: "Do not when thou art Bishop of Geneva walk in my footsteps, but defend the privileges of the Church and the freedom of the city." Pierre, of course, promised, and for a while remembered his promise, but soon forgot it, neglected Geneva, alienated its citizens, lived isolated among them, absented himself, and allowed the fruit to ripen which the House of Savoy hoped soon to pluck and eat.

This policy was attended with mixed results, some of which may be described as foreseen and desired by the ducal House; others as unforeseen and undesired, yet inevitable. We may reckon in the former class the weakening of the episcopal authority, the isolation of the Bishop, and his inability to stand alone, which meant his increased dependence on the strong arm of the Duke; and in the latter class the effect upon the people and the uprising of fit and fearless leaders. Geneva might abut upon Savoyard territory, but its citizens were not Savoyards, and did not intend to become what they were not. Around them was Swiss freedom, before them the French soil and spirit. They breathed the air, partook of the temper, lived by the help, of both; and they would be neither alienated from their kin nor cease to be masters of their own destinies. They were not dissatisfied with their Church nor with their city or its laws; they knew what they owed to the Bishop, how defenceless they would have been without him, and what immunities his presence and influence had secured. But they would not because of past favours submit to present wrongs, especially to the wrong which the freeborn man most resents, the loss of his freedom. Hence, Geneva read the situation with other eyes than the House of Savoy, and resolved not to change its religion but to preserve its liberty.

Its leaders were men like Philibert Berthelier, a genuine Genevan, self-indulgent, not free from vice, but brave, prudent, patriotic, by his death helping to redeem the city he loved; Bezanson Hugues, a statesman, pure and high-minded, incapable of meanness or cowardice, a devout Catholic, yet a strenuous republican, whose policy was to check the Savoyard by a Swiss confederacy or a joint citizenship with Swiss allies; François de Bonivard, Abbot of St Victor, a humanist with the gift of speech and of letters, a kind of provincial Erasmus, with a graphic pen and a faculty for witty epigram, yet with a courage that neither the fear nor the experience of a prison could damp. The patriots were known as "*Eyguenots*," confederates, men who had bound themselves by an oath to stand together and serve the common cause; the Savoyard party were termed "Mamelukes" because, as Bonivard tells us, "they surrendered freedom and the public weal that they might submit to tyranny, as the Mamelukes denied Christ that they might follow Mohammad."

The battle was fought with splendid tenacity; the patriots, as became loyal Catholics, first tried to coerce the Bishop by appeals to Rome and Vienne, and failed. Left face to face with Savoy, they appealed to their Swiss neighbours, Bern and Freiburg, proposed to them a joint citizenship, and long negotiated concerning it in vain. Bern hung back; for, progressive and Protestant, it did not desire that the defeat of the Duke should be to the advantage of the Bishop, who at last himself took the decisive step. On August 20, 1530, Pierre de la Baume proclaimed the Genevans rebels, and called upon the Savoyard host to put down the rebellion. Bern and Freiburg took the field, and the emancipation of Geneva began. Yet it was only a beginning; the ecclesiastical question was involved in the political, though the political had till now concealed the religious. But the revolt against the Bishop could not but become a revolt against the Church. In other times it might have been the reverse, but not now. Reform was in the air; the preachers had long stormed at the gates of the city, and they had remained closed. But with Bern helping in the front they could be kept fast no longer. They were opened, and Guillaume Farel, fiery and eloquent in speech and indomitable in spirit, preached in his fearless way. On February 8, 1534, the public opinion of Geneva pronounced for the Bernese joint citizenship, and therefore for the Reformation; and thus ended the reign of the Bishop and the chances of the House of Savoy. On May 21, 1536, the citizens of Geneva swore that they would live according to the holy Evangelical law and word of God; and two months later Calvin's connexion with the city began.

Calvin's life from this point onwards falls into three parts: his first stay in Geneva from July, 1536, to March, 1538; his residence in Strassburg from September, 1538, to September, 1541; and his second stay in Geneva from the last date till his death, May 27, 1564. In the first period, he, in company with Farel, made an attempt to organise the Church, and reform the mind and manners of Geneva, and failed; his exile, formally voted by the Council, was the penalty of his failure. In the second period he was professor of theology and French preacher at Strassburg, a trusted divine and adviser, a delegate to the Protestant Churches of Germany, which he learned to know better, making the acquaintance of Melanchthon, and becoming more appreciative of Luther. At Strassburg some of his best literary work was done—his *Letter to Cardinal Sadoleto* (in its way his most perfect production), his *Commentary on the Romans*, a *Treatise on the Lord's Supper*, the second Latin and the first French edition of his *Institutio*. In the third period he introduced and completed his legislation at Geneva, taught, preached, and published there, watched the Churches everywhere, and conducted the most extensive correspondence of his day. In these twenty-eight years he did a work which changed the face of Christendom.

It has been a subject of perhaps equal reproach among his enemies and praise by his friends that, as Beza says, Calvin "in doctrine made scarcely any change." For a young man at twenty-six to reach his final conclusions in the realms of thought and belief, especially after a radical revolution of mind, would be matter of congratulation for his enemies rather than for his admirers. But the judgment rests on a double mistake, biographical and historical. As a matter of fact, few men may have changed less; but few also have developed more. Every crisis in his career taught him something, and so enhanced his capacity. His studies of Stoicism showed him the value of morals; and he learned how to emphasise the sterner ethical qualities as well as the humaner, and the more clement by the side of the higher, public virtues. His early humanism made him a scholar and an exegete, a master of elegant Latinity, of lucid and incisive speech, of a graphic pen and historical imagination. His juristic studies gave him an idea of law, through which he interpreted the more abstract notions of theology, and a love of order, which compelled him to organise his Church. His imagination, playing upon the primitive Christian literature, helped him to see the religion Jesus instituted as Jesus Himself saw it; while the forces visible around him—the superstitions, the regnant and unreproved vices, the people so quickly sinning and so easily forgiven, the relics so innumerable and so fictitious, the acts and articles of worship, and especially the Sacraments deified and turned into substitutes for Deity—induced him to judge the system that claimed to be the sole interpreter and representative of Christ as a crafty compound of falsehood and truth.

His knowledge that the system had profited by men like Erasmus, whose wit made havoc of clerical sins and monkish superstition and Romish errors, and who yet conformed, or men like Gerard Roussel, who preached what he himself and they thought the Gospel, and who yet consented to hold office in the Catholic Church,—begat in him the belief that only by separation and negation could Reformation be accomplished. His friendship with the good and simple, those who had tried to realise the religion of Jesus, and his knowledge of the tyrannies, the miseries, and the martyrdoms which they had in consequence endured, persuaded him that his duty as an honest man was to side with the oppressed whom he admired against the oppressors whose ways and policy he detested. His experiences as a teacher and preacher of the new faith, especially at Geneva, where he tells us he found at his first coming preachings and tumults, breaking and burning of images, but no Reformation, showed him that individual men and even a whole society might profess the Reformed faith without being reformed in character. Out of these experiences came his master problem, namely, by what means could we best secure the expression of a changed faith in a changed life? Or, in other words, how could the Church be made not simply an institution for the worship of God, but an agency for the making of men fit to worship Him?

His attempt to solve this problem constitutes his chief title to a place in the history of religion and civilisation It means that Calvin was greater as a legislator than as a theologian, that we have less cause to be grateful to him for the system called Calvinism than for the Church that he organised. In other words, his polity is a more perfect expression of the man than his theology, though his theology was the point where he was most vulnerable, and where therefore he was most fiercely, not to say ferociously, attacked. The foes born in his own household, men like Castellio or Bolsec, took the Divine decrees as the spot where they could strike most fatally at him and his preeminence. The Jesuits developed their doctrine in explicit antithesis to his; and the Lutherans, when they wished to discredit his views on the Lord's Supper, thought they could do it most effectually by criticising the absolute Predestination. The sects that rose within the Reformed Church, such as the Socinian and the Remonstrant, justified their schism as a protest against views which they described as equally dishonouring to God and belittling to man. But though Calvin's theology occasioned the hottest and bitterest controversies known to Christian history, yet it is here that his mind is least original and his ideas are most clearly derivative. Without Augustine we should never have had Calvinism, which is but the principles of the anti-Pelagian treatises developed, systematised, and applied.

There are indeed two points of difference between them; Augustine disguised his positions in a criticism of hated and feared sectaries; but Calvin stated his in their severe and colossal nakedness as the sole truth which Scripture had revealed to men. Yet Augustine affirms and argues his doctrines with a breadth and a positive harshness which we do not find in Calvin; on the contrary, there is evidence that while the system held and awed Calvin's reason it yet did not win his heart. That it was taught by the greatest Father of the Church was a reason that appealed to him as a scholar; that this Father found it in Paul was a more cogent reason still, for thus it appealed to him as a thinker whose ultimate authority was the Word of God. And on this point we have incidental evidence. In August, 1539, Calvin wrote the Preface to the second edition of his *Institutio*, where the doctrines of Grace and Sin occupy for the first time their determinative position in his system; and in October of the same year he published his *Commentary on Romans*. It seems, therefore, as if the greater prominence that he now gave to the doctrines, which we have come to think most characteristic of him, was due to his closer study of Paul as interpreted by Augustine. And this system helped him to do two things: to explain his own as a normal human experience, and to face undismayed the strength and the terrors of an infallible Church. These two positions are affirmed and coordinated in a splendid passage in the *Letter to Sadoleto*, published also in 1539, in September, just between the *Institutio* and the *Commentary*, which tells of his vocation by God, and of his consequent right to speak in the name of Him who had put His word in his mouth and written His law upon his conscience. God had called him, and laid upon him a duty which he could not evade without defying God.

But here emerges another point of distinction from Augustine: Calvin conceived that God spoke to him directly, without any intermediate person or institution. Augustine's theology was absolute, but his theory of the Church was conditional, and thus the one qualified the other: the God whom the thinker conceived was modified by the God of whom the priest was the representative and mouthpiece. It is the essence of the priestly idea to manipulate and administer the conditions on which God finds access to men, and men gain access to God. Hence, so long as Augustine's theology was embedded in a sacerdotal system, the system softened the theology; the thought was accommodated to the institution, the institution was not subdued to the likeness of the thought. But Calvin rejected the Church of Augustine, and took over his later intellectual system in all its naked severity. The sin of man confronted the grace of God; man, sinful by nature, could do no right: God, infinite in majesty and in holiness, could do no wrong. Man was born in sin; his nature was corrupt, and as his nature was his actions must be. If then he was to be saved, God must save him; and, as God's will was gracious, saving was as natural to Him as sinning was to man.

Hence, we could contribute nothing towards our own salvation; God did it all; we had no merit, and He had all the glory. In a system so conceived there was no room for the priest; his prayers and sacrifices, his masses and absolutions, his shrines and relics and articles of worship, were but the impertinences of ephemeral and feeble man in the face of the Eternal Potency.

Calvin knew well the sublimity of the system which he expounded, but he could have wished it to be more pitiful. He did not love to think of the innumerable millions of the heathen with their infant children ordained to everlasting death; the decree that fixed the number alike of the saved and the lost was to him an awful decree, but he could not look towards the Alps without feeling how closely the sublime and the awful were allied. And if the sublimity of earth was terrible, how much more terrible must be the majesty of God! But if He is so august, must we not labour to attain the dignity of moral manhood, the only dignity which it becomes Him to recognise?

We come then to Calvin's legislative achievements as his main title to name and fame. But two points must here be noted. In the first place, while his theology was less original and effective than his legislation or polity, yet he so construed the former as to make the latter its logical and indeed inevitable outcome. The polity was a deduction from the theology, which may be defined as a science of the Divine will as a moral will, aiming at the complete moralisation of Man, whether as a unit or as a society. The two were thus so organically connected that each lent strength to the other, the system to the Church and the Church to the system, while other and more potently reasonable theologies either died or lived a feeble and struggling life. Secondly, the legislation was made possible and practicable by Geneva, probably the only place in Europe where it could have been enacted and enforced. We have learned enough concerning Genevan history and institutions to understand why this should have been the case. The city was small, free, homogeneous, distinguished by a strong local patriotism, a stalwart communal life. In obedience to these instincts it had just emancipated itself from the ecclesiastical Prince and its ancient religious system; and the change thus accomplished was, though disguised in a religious habit, yet essentially political. For the Council which abolished the Bishop had made itself heir to his faculties and functions; it could only dismiss him as civil lord by dismissing him as the ecclesiastical head of Geneva, and in so doing it assumed the right to succeed as well as to supersede him in both capacities. This, however, involved a notable inversion of old ideas; before the change the ecclesiastical authority had been civil, but because of the change the civil authority became ecclesiastical. If theocracy means the rule of the Church or the sovereignty of the clergy in the State, then the ancient constitution of Geneva was theocratic; if democracy means the sovereignty of the people in Church as well as in

State, then the change had made it democratic. And it was just after the change had been effected that Calvin's connexion with the city began.

Its chief pastor had persuaded him to stay as a colleague, and the Council appointed him professor and preacher. He was young, exactly twenty-seven years of age, full of high ideals, but inexperienced, unacquainted with men, without any knowledge of Geneva and the state of things there. He could therefore make no terms, could only stay to do his duty. What that duty was soon became apparent. Geneva had not become any more moral in character because it had changed its mind in religion. It had two months before Calvin's arrival sworn to live according to the holy evangelical law and Word of God; but it did not seem to understand its own oath. And the man whom his intellectual sincerity and moral integrity had driven out of Catholicism, could not hold office in any Church which made light of conviction and conduct; and so he at once set himself to organise a Church that should be efficaciously moral. He built on the ancient Genevan idea, that the city is a Church; only he wished to make the Church to be primary and real. The theocracy, which had been construed as the reign of the clergy, he would interpret as ideal and realise as a reign of God. The citizens, who had assumed control of their own spiritual destinies and ecclesiastical affairs, he wanted to instruct in their responsibilities and discipline into obedience. And he would do it in the way of a jurist who believes in the harmony of law and custom; he would by positive enactments train the city, which conceived itself to be a Church, to be and behave as if it were indeed a Church, living according to the Gospel which it had sworn to obey.

Thus a confession of faith was drawn up which the people were to adopt as their own, and so attain clarity and concordance of mind concerning God and His Word; and a catechism was composed which was to be made the basis of religious instruction in both the school and the family, for the citizen as well as the child. Worship was to be carefully regulated, psalm-books prepared, psalm-singing cultivated; the preacher was to interpret the Word, and the pastor to supervise the flock. The Lord's Supper was to be celebrated monthly, but only those who were morally fit or worthy were to be allowed to communicate. The Church, in order that it might fulfil its functions and guard the Holy Table, must have the right of excommunication. It was not enough that a man should be a citizen or a councillor to be admitted to the Lord's Supper; his mind must be Christian, and his conduct Christ-like. Without faith the rite was profaned, the presence of Christ was not realised. Moreover, since matrimonial cases were many and infelicity sprang both from differences of faith and impurity of conduct, a board, composed partly of magistrates and partly of ministers, was to be appointed to deal with them; and it was to have the power to exclude from the Church those who either did not believe its doctrines or did not obey its commandments.

These were drastic proposals to be made to a city which had just dismissed its Bishop, attained political freedom, and proclaimed a Reformation of religion; and Calvin was not the man to leave them inoperative. A card-player was pilloried; a tire-woman, a mother, and two bridesmaids were arrested because they had adorned the bride too gaily; an adulterer was driven with the partner of his guilt through the streets by the common hangman, and then banished. These things taxed the temper of the city sorely; it was not unfamiliar with legislation of the kind, but it had not been accustomed to see it enforced. Hence, men who came to be known as "libertines," though they were both patriotic and moral and only craved freedom, rose and said, "This is an intolerable tyranny; we will not allow any man to be lord over our consciences." And about the same time Calvin's orthodoxy was challenged. Two Anabaptists arrived and demanded liberty to prophesy; and Peter Caroli charged him with heresy as to the Trinity. He would not use the Athanasian Creed; and he defended himself by reasons that the scholar who knows its history will respect. The end soon came. When he heard that he had been sentenced to banishment, he said, "If I had served men this would have been a poor reward, but I have served Him who never fails to perform what He has promised."

In 1541 Geneva recalled Calvin, and he obeyed as one who goes to fulfil an imperative but unwelcome duty. There is nothing more pathetic in the literature of the period than his hesitancies and fears. He tells Farel that he would rather die a hundred times than again take up that cross "*in qua millies quotidie pereundum esset.*" And he writes to Viret that it were better to perish once for all than "*in illa carnificina iterum torqueri.*" But he loved Geneva, and it was in evil case. Rome was plotting to reclaim it; Savoy was watching her opportunity, the patriots feared to go forward, and even the timid dared not go back. So the necessities of the city, divided between its factions and its foes, constituted an appeal which Calvin could not resist; but he did not yield unconditionally. He went back as the legislator who was to frame laws for its Church; and he so adapted them to the civil constitution and the constitution to them, that he raised the little city of Geneva to be the Protestant Rome.

Calvin's idea, whether of the Church or the State, it is neither possible nor necessary to discuss fully here; as he conceived, Fatherhood belonged to God, motherhood to the Church: we entered into life by being conceived in her womb and suckled at her breasts, and so long as we lived we were as scholars in her school. She was catholic, holy, one and indivisible; to invent another Church would be to divide Christ. In this sense she comprehended all the people of God, His elect in every age and place; but this eternal and internal Church was, as it were, distributed into local and external Churches, which existed in the towns and villages inhabited of men. Calvin held, indeed, that the local ought to possess the same spiritual qualities as the universal Church; but he did not hold the two to be identical. They differed in many ways; in the one case the chosen of God constituted the Church, but in the other case, as Augustine had said, "there are very many sheep without, and very many wolves within." The universal Church lived under the immediate sovereignty of God; but particular Churches, while bound so to live, yet were organised according to the wants of human society, and so long as the people were God's and lived unto Him, their society was a Church, which, as an inhabitant of space and time, could not but live its corporate life in some State, in relation to it even while differing from it. What this relation ought to be Calvin rather implied than discussed. He assumed their distinctness, but his policy often involved their identity. It would be approximately true to say that the ideal Church was independent of the State, above it while distributed through it; but the actual Church, while owing its existence to the ideal, was yet associated with the State, and often bound to act with it and through it. It was not possible that a local Church should be merged in the State, for then it would cease to be a Divine institution; or be subordinate to the State, for then it would be a mere minister of man's will, subject to all the accidents and influences proper to time; or be separated from the State, for then it would be cut off from the field which most needed its presence and action.

Hence the proper analogy was natural rather than political:—as soul and body constituted one man, so Church and State constituted one society, distinct in function but inseparable in being. Without the State there would be no medium for the Church to work in, no body for the soul to animate; without the Church there would be no law higher than expediency to govern the State, no ideal of thought and conduct, no soul to animate the body. Both Church and State therefore were necessary to the good ordering of society, and each was explained by the same idea. All human authority was the creation of God; His will had formed the State to care for the actual man, who was temporal, and the Church to care for the ideal man, who was immortal. Each had the same cause or root; and, without both, life could not be so ordered as to realise Eternal Will. Over the State God placed the magistrate, who might here be a monarch, an Emperor or King, and there a Syndic or Council, created by the people for the people; but whatever he might be, he was yet a power ordained of God for the good of man and the regulation of society. In, rather than over, the Church God had set a ministry or authorities that were to rule by the teaching which convinced the reason and commanded the conscience, and by the service which won the heart and persuaded the will. The ministers were responsible to the State in all civil matters; but the magistrates were responsible to the Church in all religious concerns, especially those affecting faith and conduct. The laws of the State were civil in form, but religious in origin; the laws of the Church were civil in sanction, though spiritual in scope and purpose. Calvin indeed had, as regards civil polity, distinguished between monarchy, aristocracy, and democracy, and had indicated their respective excellences and defects, as well as his own personal preferences; but he declined to assert that one of them was absolutely or under all conditions the best. He could not feel as if a similar latitude of judgment were allowed him as regards the Church, where man was not free to follow any order he liked, for in the New Testament a polity was given him to imitate. Our Lord had Himself shown how His Church ought to be governed, and where He had spoken man's duty was to interpret His word and do His will.

The *Ordonnances Ecclésiastiques* may be described as Calvin's programme of Genevan reform, or his method for applying to the local and external Church the government which our Lord had instituted and the Apostles had realised. These Ordinances expressed his historical sense and gratified his religious temper, while adapting the Church to the city, so that the city might become a better Church. To explain in detail how he proposed to do this is impossible within our limits; and we shall therefore confine ourselves to the most important of the factors he created, the Ministry and the Consistory.

The Reformed ministry had till now been largely the creation of conversion, or inspiration, or chance, and the result could not be termed satisfactory. Convinced men had found their way into it, and had created a conviction as sincere and an enthusiasm as vehement as their own; but along with them had also come hosts of restless men, moved by superficial and often ignoble causes:—discontent, petulance, discomfort, the desire to legitimise illegitimate connexions, dislike to authority, and the mere love of change. And they had proved most mischievous forces in the Protestant Churches, had continued restless, become seditious, impracticable, schismatic, authors of disorder and enemies of peace, who arrested progress and made men ashamed of change. Calvin had had his own experience of these men; and he, as a man of grave and juristic mind, had found the experience disagreeable, and was to find it more disagreeable still. With the insight of genius he perceived that the battle could be won, not by chance recruits, but only by a disciplined army; and, in order that the army might be created, he invented the discipline. The Ordinances may indeed be termed a method for making and guiding a Reformed ministry, a clergy that, without any priestly character, should yet be more efficient than the ancient priesthood. Hence where the Roman placed the Church, Calvin set the Deity, and made a man's right to enter the ministerial office depend on his vocation by God. But this belief in a Divine choice and call was to be tested by a threefold process, Examination, Election, Institution or Introduction. The Examination, which was to be conducted by men already in the ministry, the recognised preachers and teachers of the Church, covered the whole period of thought and life; what the candidate had learned at school and college, what he had been at home and in society, what evidence he could furnish as to his call being of God. He had to show what and why he believed; the relation in which his beliefs stood to the Church on the one hand and the Scriptures on the other; whether he could teach what he had learned, or preach as he believed; how he had hitherto lived, and whether he had so behaved himself as to be without reproach. If the candidate satisfied the ministerial examiners, they presented him to the Council; if the Council approved, he preached before the people; and if they approved, he was declared to be elected a minister of the Word. Institution, which was as much a civil as a religious process, followed, and it ended with the candidate taking an oath before the Council that he would edify the Church, serve the city, and set to all a goodly example of obedience.

But these initial steps were not the most essential parts of the discipline; more effectual still were the means employed to secure the minister's efficiency, and to define his relation to the city or Church. The conduct of each person was the concern of the ministerial body as a whole; and the behaviour of the body was open to the criticism of every minister. The humblest pastor had the right, which was laid upon him as a duty, to criticise the bearing or the action of the most eminent; and responsibility was so personal and yet so collective, at once so concentrated and so distributed, that while it belonged to all, each individual was made to feel as if he alone bore it. Thus in Geneva the ministers formed the Venerable Company, correspondent to the Smaller Council, which was, as it were, the cabinet or executive of the Greater; and every week it met in Congregation, as it was called, to study the Scriptures, discuss doctrine, and review conduct. There was, besides, every three months a special Synod which made inquisition into the faults and failures of the brotherhood, and was charged with the discipline of the faithless. Alongside of these faculties ran duties which were coextensive with the religious wants of the city. The minister of the Word was a preacher who had to speak to the people concerning the truth and will of God; a pastor of the flock which was given him to supervise and tend; a guide of the worship which he was bound to make worthy of God and uplifting to man; an administrator of the Sacraments which sealed the covenants and spoke to faith of God's saving grace and the presence of His Son; an instructor with the duty of catechising old and young and directing education; a friend to every man who needed him, with a special mission to the poor, especially in seasons of disease and distress, while also the soul of all the charity in the city.

Nor, though the ministers were to hold so influential a place in the body politic, could they come to feel as if they were a self-propagating, an exclusive, or a sacrosanct corporation. Without the ministry the minister could not be made; but without the people he could not be called or maintained. He issued from the ranks of the citizens, and he could be reduced to their condition again. If his conduct was scandalous, or if his faith changed or failed, the reduction was inevitable. He was responsible to the Church, typified by its clergy; and responsible for the Church, typified by the city or the laity. Calvin's theory was a theocracy, not a hierocracy; the clergy did not reign, nor did the organised Church govern; but God reigned over Church and State alike, and so governed that both magistrates and clergy were His ministers. In Geneva every office was sacred, and existed for the glory of the God who was its Creator.

The ministerial ideal embodied in these Ecclesiastical Ordinances may be said to have had certain indirect but international results; it compelled Calvin to develop his system of education; it supplied the Reformed Church, especially in France, with the men which it needed to fight its battles and to form the iron in its blood; it presented the Reformed Church everywhere with an intellectual and educational ideal which must be realised if its work was to be done; and it created the modern preacher, defining the sphere of his activity and setting up for his imitation a noble and lofty example.

Calvin soon found that the Reformed faith could live in a democratic city only by an enlightened pulpit speaking to enlightened citizens, and that an educated ministry was helpless without an educated people. His method for creating both entitles him to rank among the foremost makers of modern education. As a humanist he believed in the classical languages and literatures—there is a tradition which says that he read through Cicero once a year—and so "he built his system on the solid rock of Græco-Roman antiquity." Yet he did not neglect religion; he so trained the boys of Geneva through his Catechism that each was said to be able to give a reason for his faith "like a doctor of the Sorbonne." He believed in the unity of knowledge and the community of learning, placing the magistrate and the minister, the citizen and the pastor, in the hands of the same teacher, and binding the school and the university together. The boy learned in the one and the man studied in the other; but the school was the way to the university, the university was the goal of the school. In nothing does the pædagogic genius of Calvin more appear than in his fine jealousy as to the character and competence whether of masters or professors, and in his unwearied quest after qualified men. His letters teem with references to the men in various lands and many universities whom he was seeking to bring to Geneva. The first Rector, Antoine Saunier, was a notable man; and he never rested till he had secured his dear old teacher, Mathurin Cordier.

Castellio was a schoolmaster; Theodore Beza was head of College and Academy, or school and university, together; and Calvin himself was a professor of theology. The success of the College was great; the success of the Academy was greater. Men came from all quarters—English, Italians, Spanish, Germans, Russians, ministers, jurists, old men, young men, all with the passion to learn in their blood—to jostle each other among the thousand hearers who met to listen to the great Reformer. But France was the main feeder of the Academy; Frenchmen filled its chairs, occupied its benches, learned in it the courage to live and the will to die. From Geneva books poured into France; and the French Church was ever appealing for ministers, yet never appealed in vain. Within eleven years, 1555–66—Calvin died in 1564—it is known that Geneva sent 161 pastors into France; how many more may have gone, unrecorded, we cannot tell. And they were learned men, strenuous, fearless, praised by a French Bishop as modest, grave, saintly, with the name of Jesus Christ ever on their lips. Charles IX implored the magistrates of Geneva to stop the supply and withdraw the men already sent; but the magistrates replied that the preachers had been sent not by them but by their ministers, who believed that the sovereign duty of all Princes and Kings was to do homage to Him who had given to them their dominion. It was small wonder that the Venetian Suriano should describe Geneva as "the mine whence came the ore of heresy"; or that the Protestants should gather courage as they heard the men from Geneva sing psalms in the face of torture and death.

It was indeed a very different France which the eyes of the dying Calvin saw from that which the young man had seen thirty years before. Religious hate was even more bitter and vindictive; war had come and made persecution more ferocious; but the Huguenots had grown numerous, potent, respected, feared, and disputed with Catholicism the supremacy of the kingdom. And Calvin had done it, not by arms nor by threats, nor by encouragement of sedition or insurrection—to such action he was ever resolutely opposed—but by the agency of the men whom he formed in Geneva, and by their persuasive speech. The Reformed minister was essentially a preacher, intellectual, exegetical, argumentative, seriously concerned with the subjects that most appealed to the serious-minded. Modern oratory may be said to begin with him, and indeed to be his creation. He helped to make the vernacular tongues of Western Europe literary. He accustomed the people to hear the gravest and most sacred themes discussed in the language which they knew; and the themes ennobled the language, the language was never allowed to degrade the themes. And there was no tongue and no people that he influenced more than the French. Calvin made Bossuet and Massillon possible; as a preacher he found his successor in Bourdaloue; and a literary critic who does not love him has expressed a doubt as to whether Pascal could be more eloquent or was so profound. And the ideal then realised in

Geneva exercised an influence far beyond France. It extended into Holland, which in the strength of the Reformed faith resisted Charles V and his son, achieved independence, and created the freest and best educated State on the continent of Europe. John Knox breathed for awhile the atmosphere of Geneva, was subdued into the likeness of the man who had made it, and when he went home he copied its education and tried to repeat its Reformation. English Reformers, fleeing from martyrdom, found a refuge within its hospitable walls, and, returning to England, attempted to establish the Genevan discipline, and failed, but succeeded in forming the Puritan character. If the author of the *Ordonnances Ecclésiastiques* accomplished, whether directly or indirectly, so much, we need not hesitate to term him a notable friend to civilisation.

The Consistory may be described as Calvin's method for moralising through the Church the life of man and the State to which he belonged. He may in the manner of the jurist have imagined that regulation by positive law was the most efficient means of governing conduct; but if he legislated as a jurist, he thought and purposed as a Reformer. It is here, where injustice is easiest, that we ought to be most scrupulously just. Calvin was resolved, so far as he had power, to make the Church what it had not been but what it ought to be, an institution organised for the creation of a moral mankind. For this reason he claimed for it the right of excommunication and the power to excommunicate. But as he conceived the matter, the exercise of the power which followed from the possession of the right, while spiritual in essence and in purpose, might yet be civil in certain of its effects. The Consistory was a body appointed to be the guardian of morals, and therefore possessed of the power to excommunicate.

It was composed of six ministers and twelve elders. The elders were to be elected annually, and were to be men of good and honourable conduct, blameless and free from suspicion, animated by the fear of God and endowed with spiritual wisdom. They were to be chosen, two from the Smaller Council, four from the Council of Sixty, and six from the Great Council; they were to be elected at the same time as the magistrates, were to be capable of re-election, and were to take the oath of allegiance to the State and fidelity to the Church. They represented the idea that Geneva was a Church-State; and their duties were to have their eyes upon every man, family, or district, to have their ears open to every complaint, to punish every offence according to a carefully-graduated scale, and to enforce purity everywhere. The Consistory's jurisdiction was not civil, but spiritual; the sword which it wielded was not Caesar's but Christ's, yet it had rights of entry and investigation that were not so much Christ's as Caesar's. It was a judicial body and sat every Thursday to examine charges of misconduct or immorality, to pass sentences from which there was no appeal, and where necessary to hand the guilty over to the magistrates to be punished according to law. If any offender refused to appear, a civil officer was sent to bring him; and so every ecclesiastical offence became an act of civil disobedience. Thus, obstinate refusal to communicate was regarded as a punishable crime; so were frivolous or continued absence from church, disrespect to parents, blasphemy, and adultery. One young woman who sang profane songs was banished, and another who sang them to psalm-tunes was scourged. Heresy became as much an offence as immorality. If a creed or confession becomes a law of the State as well as of the Church, to speak or agitate against it becomes treason. In other words, if opinion is established by law, heresy is turned into crime. And this Geneva soon discovered. Castellio's doubts as to the canonicity of Solomon's Song, and as to the received interpretation of Christ's descent into Hades, Bolsec's criticism of predestination, Gruet's suspected scepticism and possession of infidel books, Servetus' rationalism and anti-Trinitarian creed, were all opinions judged to be criminal. Infallibility is not the only system that makes heresy culpable and the heretic guilty. If the Church will be a State, and enforce its laws, which must affect both conduct and belief, by the only method a State can follow, then it must bear the reproach of being more cruel, and therefore more unjust, than any purely civil power. The heretic may be a man of irreproachable character; but if heresy be treason against the law, a character without reproach may aggravate rather than extenuate the crime. The man of imperfect morals may be too feeble of will to differ in opinion from the constituted authority, and his intellectual conformity may save him from the sentence which his moral weakness deserves. And time alone was needed to make it obvious how imperfectly Geneva could attain either unity of faith or purity of life by turning her Church into a city governed by positive law.

Many points remain of necessity undiscussed. The merits and defects of Calvin as a writer of polemical treatises; his work as a statesman, and his appreciation of political questions in lands so unlike his own as England; his qualities as a correspondent who feels no affairs of State too large to grapple with, and no personal concern too small to touch; his worth and wisdom as an adviser who loves the great of the earth for the good they can do, and judges that the higher a person is placed the more need there is for plain and candid speech, but who forgets not the humble and the poor, and can pause amid the mightiest concerns to hear their plaints; his attachment and tenderness as a friend, whether in his brilliant youth or his sadder age, when he loved to unbosom himself to his strenuous comrade Guillaume Farel, or his devoted companion Pierre Viret—could have justice done them only were the limits of our space wholly different from what they are.

But there are three things that may be emphasised in conclusion. The first is Calvin's irenical services to Protestantism. He made the Reformed Church less antithetical to the Lutheran, and the Lutheran leaders better understood among the Reformed. His doctrine of the Lord's Supper may be described as a spiritual doctrine of the Real Presence; he escaped the miserable perplexities which lurked in the scholastic notion of *Substantia*, and were used to justify Transubstantiation on the one hand, and Consubstantiation on the other. Where faith was, there the Lord was, and where it was not there could be no idea of Him, and no image or symbol could speak of His presence. Secondly, mention must be made of Calvin's services to the French tongue. He perhaps more than any other man made it a literary vehicle, a medium for high philosophical and religious discussion. The *Institutio* has been said to be the first book written in French which can be described as logically composed, built up according to a consecutive and proportioned plan. The style is the man, exact, sober, precise, restrained; sad perhaps, or a trifle cold, but full of conviction and reason. The French he speaks is a natural product, an evolution and a new phase of the medieval French, refreshed, vivified, made simpler and more living by baptism in its original source, classical Latinity. Thirdly, his services to the cause of sacred learning must not be forgotten. These it is hardly possible to exaggerate; he is the sanest of commentators, the most skilled of exegetes, the most reasonable of critics. He knows how to use an age to interpret a man, a man to interpret an age. His exegesis is never forced or fantastic; he is less rash and subjective in his judgments than Luther; more reverent to Scripture, more faithful to history, more modern in spirit. His work on the Psalms has much to make our most advanced scholars ashamed of the small progress we have made either in method or in conclusions. And his work is inspired by a noble belief; he thought that the one way to realise Christianity was by knowing the mind of Christ; that this mind was expressed in the Scriptures; and that to make them living and credible was to make indefinitely more possible its incorporation in the thoughts and institutions of man. It is by his service to this cause that Calvin must be ultimately judged.

www.ingramcontent.com/pod-product-compliance
Lightning Source LLC
Chambersburg PA
CBHW061311040426
42444CB00010B/2589